Jerry Yang

Jennifer Strand

abdopublishing.com

Published by Abdo Zoom™, PO Box 398166, Minneapolis, Minnesota 55439.

Printed in the United States of America, North Mankato, Minnesota
102016
012017

Cover Photo: Paul Sakuma/AP Images
Interior Photos: Paul Sakuma/AP Images, 1, 4, 9, 19; Don Ryan/AP Images, 5; iStockphoto, 6–7; Seth Poppel/Yearbook Library, 7; Evan Lorne/Shutterstock Images, 10; Simon Kwong/Reuters/Newscom, 12; Marcio Jose Sanchez/AP Images, 13; Gregory Bull/AP Images, 14–15; Itsuo Inouye/AP Images, 16; Ahmad Faizal Yahya/Shutterstock Images, 17

Editor: Brienna Rossiter
Series Designer: Madeline Berger
Art Direction: Dorothy Toth

Publisher's Cataloging-in-Publication Data
Names: Strand, Jennifer, author.
Title: Jerry Yang / by Jennifer Strand.
Description: Minneapolis, MN : Abdo Zoom, 2017. | Series: Technology pioneers | Includes bibliographical references and index.
Identifiers: LCCN 2016948916 | ISBN 9781680799293 (lib. bdg.) | ISBN 9781624025150 (ebook) | 9781624025716 (Read-to-me ebook)
Subjects: LCSH: Yang, Jerry, 1968- --Juvenile literature. | Telecommunications engineers--United States--Biography--Juvenile literature. | Computer programmers--United States--Biography--Juvenile literature. | Webmasters--United States--Biography--Juvenile literature.
Classification: DDC 338.7/6102504092 [B]--dc23
LC record available at http://lccn.loc.gov/2016948916

Table of Contents

Introduction

Jerry Yang helped create Yahoo!

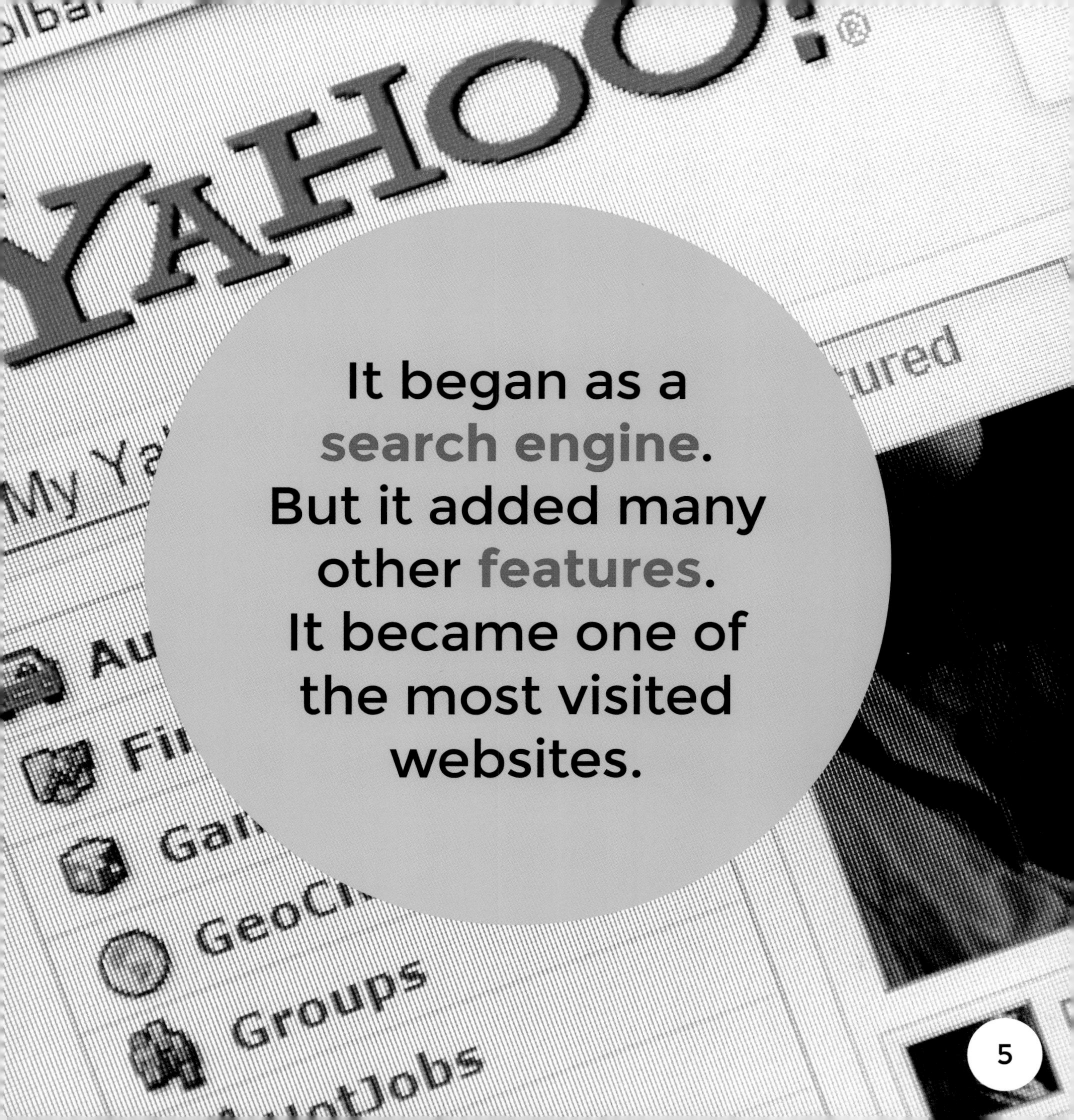

It began as a **search engine**. But it added many other **features**. It became one of the most visited websites.

Early Life

Jerry was born on November 6, 1968. His family was from Taiwan.

They moved to the United States when Jerry was ten.

Leader

Yang studied computers. At this time it was hard to find things online. Yang and his friend David Filo made a search engine. It helped find websites they liked.

Other people could use it, too. They typed in **keywords**. The search engine showed them a list of related websites.

This made it much easier for people to find the websites they wanted. Soon many people were using Yahoo!

Career

Yang and Filo
started Yahoo! Inc. in 1995.

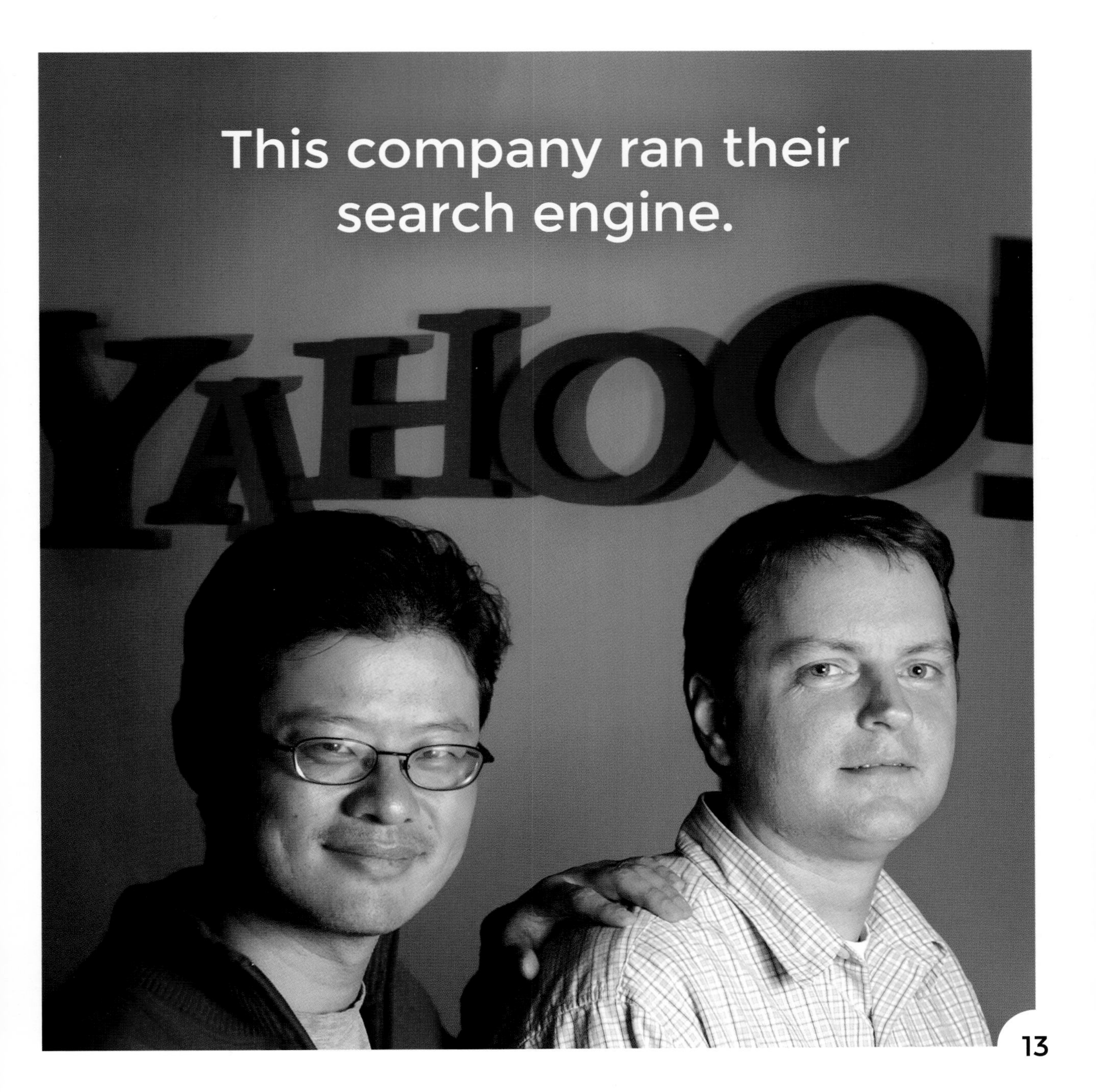

This company ran their search engine.

Soon they added news stories and an e-mail service.

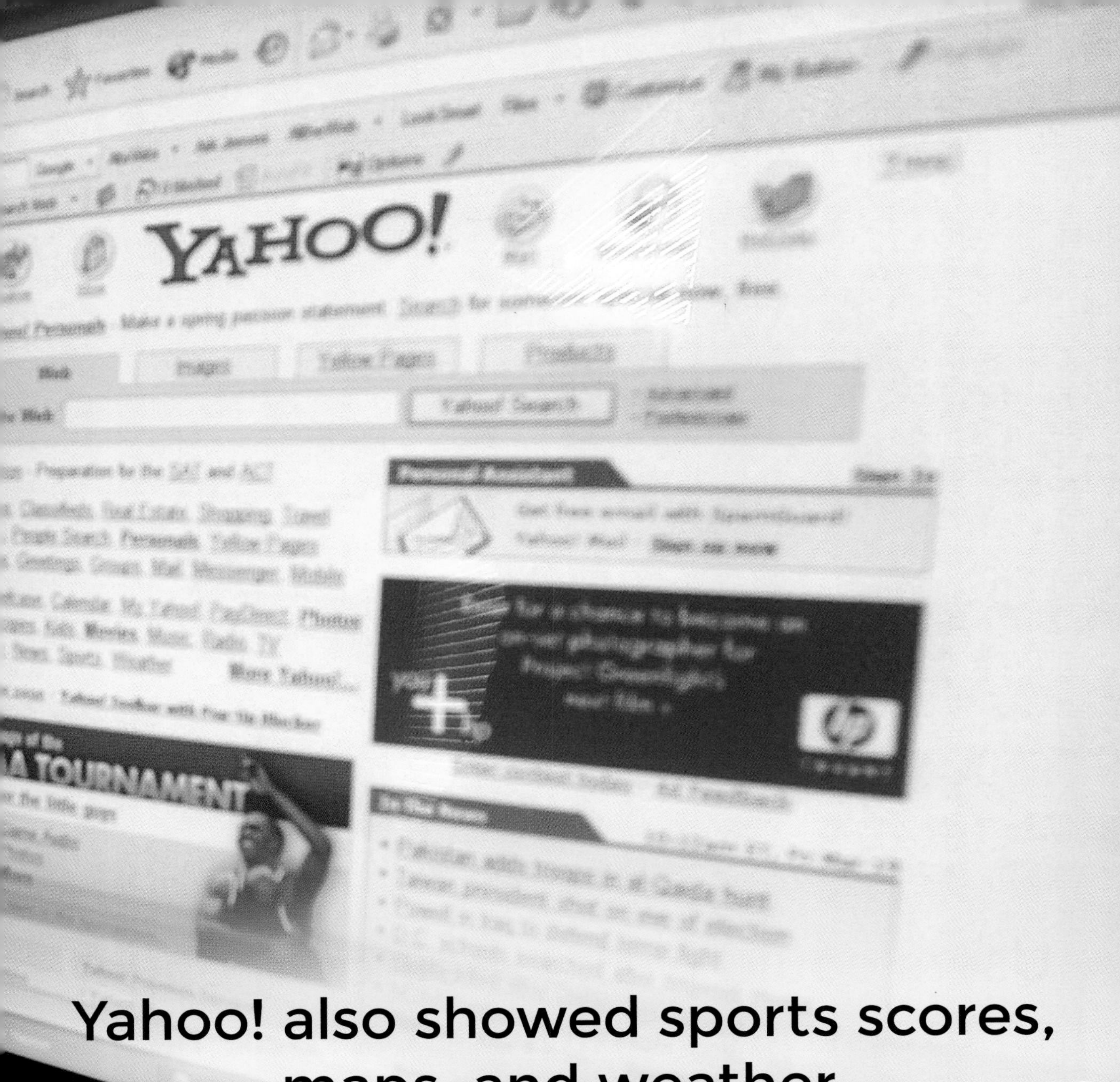

Yahoo! also showed sports scores, maps, and weather.

Users could make their own page, too. They could **customize** it.

They chose the information and links they wanted to see.

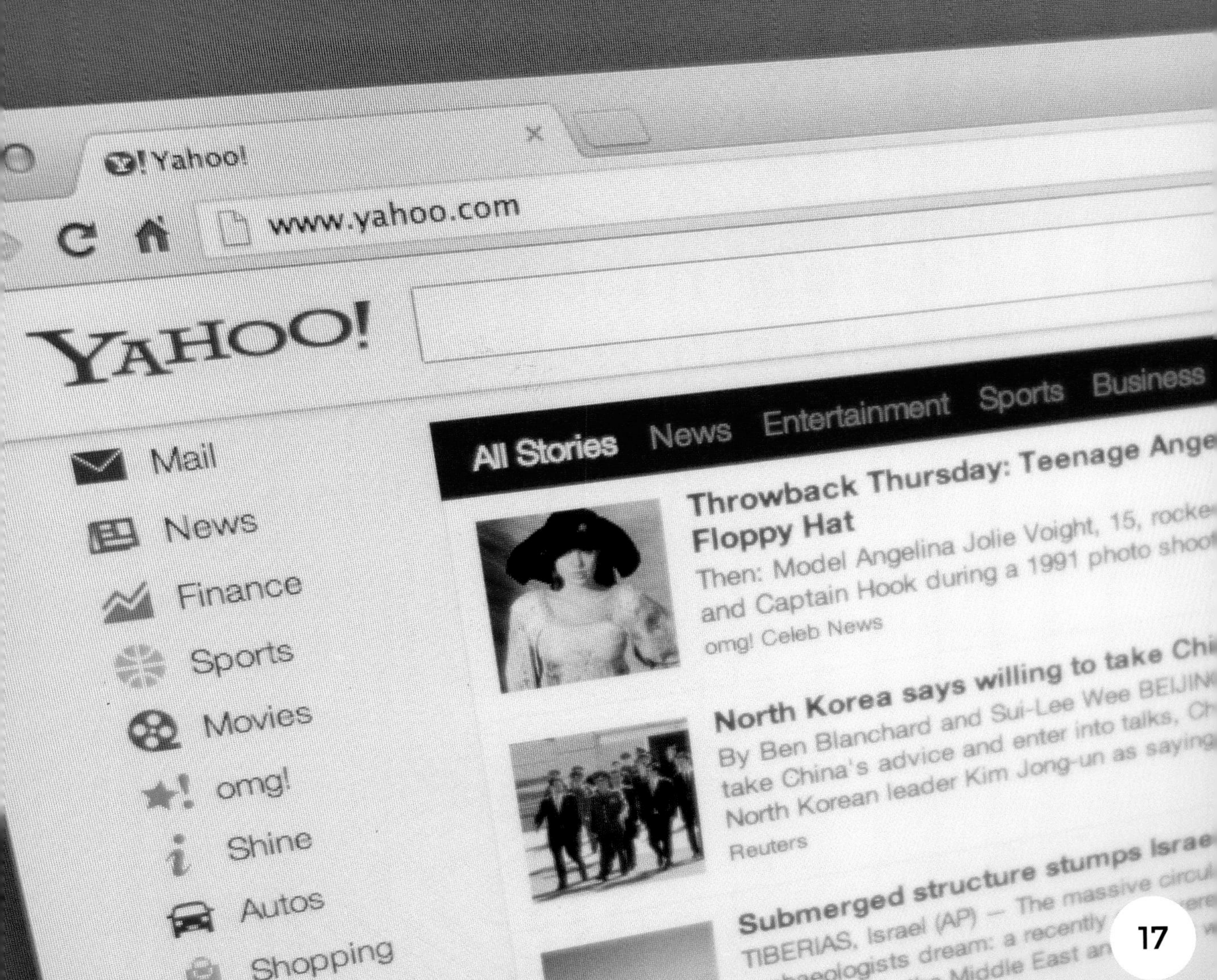

Legacy

Yahoo! made it easy for people to find things online. At one time, the company was worth $130 billion.

Jerry Yang

Born: November 6, 1968

Birthplace: Taipei, Taiwan

Wife: Akiko Yamazaki

Known For: Yang helped create a popular search engine. He was a cofounder of Yahoo! Inc.

1968: Jerry Yang is born on November 6.

1978: Yang's family moves to the United States.

1994: Yang and David Filo create their search engine.

1995: Yang and Filo found Yahoo! Inc.

1999: The *MIT Technology Review* names Yang one of the world's top 100 innovators under age 35.

2007–2009: Yang is the CEO of Yahoo! Inc.

Glossary

customize - change to fit a person's wants or needs.

feature - an important part or characteristic of something.

keyword - a word used to find websites or information about a specific topic.

link - a connection from one website to another website.

search engine - a program that searches the Internet and shows a list of results.

Booklinks

For more information
on Jerry Yang, please visit
booklinks.abdopublishing.com

Zoom™ In on Biographies!

Learn even more with the Abdo Zoom Biographies database. Check out abdozoom.com for more information.

Index